The Fear of Algebra

The Fear of Algebra

Jed Allen

Mulberry
Knoll
BOOKS FOR US
Fairfield, Iowa USA

Mulberry Knoll
508 W. Jackson Ave.
Fairfield, IA
USA 52556-3541

www.mulberryKnoll.com

First Mulberry Knoll edition 2011.

Publisher Catologing-in-Publication Data:

Allen, Jed

The Fear of Algebra: poems. — 1st Mulberry Knoll ed.
116 pages.   0.75cm.
ISBN-10   0-9792104-1-0
ISBN-13   978-0-9792104-1-9
1. Literature   I. Title.   II. Poetry.

811.5

Printed in the United States of America.

DEDICATION

These writings are for Carol Barber LaCroix.

We are not wolves, but lambs astonished in the
margins of the fields by sunlight and summer.

Sebastian Barry

All this is foul smell and blood in a bag.

Marcus Aurelius

ACKNOWLEDGMENTS

Some of these poems, sometimes in earlier versions, appeared in *Hayden's Ferry Review, Chiron, Green Mountains Review,* the *Marlboro Review, Fever Dreams: contemporary arizona poets,* ed. Leilani Wright and James V. Cervantes (University of Arizona Press, 1997), *Main Street Rag Poetry Journal, Alligator Juniper, Red Night, The Salt River Review, Maverick, Borborygmus, Poet Lore, Aktion, Bootlick, Gila River Review,* and *Merge Poetry Journal.*

CONTENTS

I

THE FEAR OF ALGEBRA

And God will start crying over my book:
these are not words—convulsions compressed into lumps.
He'll run through the sky, my poems in his hands,
and, spluttering, show them to his friends.

Vladimir Mayakovsky

THE FEAR OF ALGEBRA

4 women huddled
at the rear

are shot through the eyes. A 5th running
toward the 4 fallen is shot

high in the chest then
twice again in the lower leg.

In the men's room, 3rd stall, 2 men
copulating are shotgunned in the mouth. Moments

later 3 boys hunched in their seats
are popped through the ears

neatly. An undetermined number—x—
of seats are spattered. Witnesses, 7 in all, 5

elderly, all indigent, sob
at the base of the spine. High

in the rigging over the stage 6 pigeons
are riddled till their wings

explode in 12 screams and every feather
floats downward

but 1. This feather is y.

Those manning the weapons are dragged
center-stage and shot in the neck. Those

shooting are shot as well
along with those who are

factoring and
generally keeping count.

Eventually nothing in the auditorium moves
but dust and y, floating.

At the same time the Hands of God
creep fingerdown along the central corridor

at a pace of 1 centimeter per 17 seconds.
The temperature plunges

3 degrees centigrade every
8 seconds. Given

the bright day, the fluids
in the men's room, the coins

still settling in the pockets of the dead—and
considering scrupulously the condition

of the generators, the tick
and shudder of 26 wall clocks in the building

and the weight, finally, in grams,
of the 1 wing feather that hesitates, drifting

down yet never reaching bottom—how long, reader,
will it take God's hands to reach us?

WALKING SONG

If I can't get in, if they turn me back, if I just can't
take another grim-grime mile of road and wind and
disemboweled trucks, if my shoes are shot, if it's too
bleak and mirky dark and sure no place for poetry, if I
stagger and stutter, too bummed, whacked out, if my hands
stink and my tools drip, if I just got free but I'm plain
chicken, my hair plucked, oh mother if I can't praise,
can't say anything good, an encouraging word—such a
nice young man—if I'm still confusing *can* and *may*, Christ
if I can't contribute, make a mark, if all's I do is slobber
and sing, if I fuck with the poem, you know, if I say it,
the word, if I go to the men, shoulder in and lay it down,
saying hey we gotta change, gotta give it up, if my knee
goes out, here on the road, if things get small, tight,
tough, if suddenly I see that all this time I'm actually
inside, in the chests of the men, in the shadow of Shadows,
the infamous Valley, jesus if they're waiting for me, real
men, if they itch, if I knock some blazing night at the
cold skull lodge and find them drunk and stooping over
the boy in a barber's chair with a dirty drain beneath and I,
True Jed, doth loom heroic in the dark door, blooming,
burning, driven to speak, not watching my back, with my
father's garters holding up my father's socks and BAM!
they pin me cool and fast, punching till I name the Presidents
—*Lincoln*—WHAM! J-Jackson—WHAM!—and they
call me college boy and a cocksucker and bust my writing
stick and dump my pail of tears or worse if they stare
right through me and I blow my lines, frantically fingering
my father's words slung around my neck—*Coolidge*—*Kennedy*
WHAM! WHAM!—if I *still* don't know the value of a dollar,
if I'm still not good to Mother, if I'm not a Great Man, if I don't
kneel, don't suck, if my shoulders are small and my dick
smaller, if my soul leaks, if I'm soft, a cunt, too hurt,
a loser, if I don't pack right, if my brain boils and my jaw
jams, if I grin like Sheriff Big, if my nose knows
the crack, if I sniff the seats when they stand, the kings
of my country—N-N-Nixon—WHAM!—man if my reals

battle and boom, if my fly sparks, if I'm shit in the sun,
if I won't do it, no, never, if I'm only a fake, a fool, semi-hard—
boys if I haven't got it, if I can't score, if
I'm bad at the net WHAM if I can't shoot WHAM can't fight
WHAM can't measure up or stare them down, if I'm really
alone and suck at math, if there's nothing but blood and
gas and the Himmelfahrt, the flash of buttocks, and me
a boy with old bones, head down, huffing, big hands
paddling, striding out of light and time—if round this
bend the road is suddenly fenced with men, if their shaved
heads shine, if they're grinning, if they're watching me, eyes
iced, sticks bristling, if the women are gone, dear god, the sun
falling, the sky roiling black, and I will never make it, striding,
my shoes done, my face in flames, shouting MAKE WAY! crying
MAKE WAY! and the road going on forever

OCTOBER, 1971

Sister:

I have this movie
running in my head

of Jed in his old suit
stoned and gawking

at the Cessna smeared
over the snowy slope

like a crushed bug—
chunks of rib and wing

flung a hundred yards—
ten bodies

spilled
in the smoky muck—

and he considers
robbing them—he's *that* bad—

father
on his back

beneath the squirming birds
—and mother, damn her,

strapped
in her seat but

slopping out
and her head

wrenched
wrongfully back—

he staggers
pukes

then hurls her purse
at the squabbling birds

and begins
to dig in her

like a dog,
her cold blood

caking under his nails—
howling down

in her broken face—she's
like a huge doll—*don't go*

oh no, not yet—
you owe us

an explanation—

and grunting he drags
the heavy flesh

through the mess
to father

and props them up
but they keep toppling

so he slips to his knees
giggling, sobbing,

to straighten mother's head
and father's smashed hands

and her rings flattened
and his watch stopped—and right then

they rise, sister—
I swear it, like a dark

sigh they drift up
blind, wordless

the two of them
trailing their gore

in the darkening haze,
a shoe falling into the birds.

Can you see him too?
Bloody hands, hippy hair.

Oh such a life, sister.

THE BODY OF GOD

Again!

I've told you: I stood in the door, key in hand, out of breath
from the stairs—I was glad to be home, my little room, my books,
all that. And there it was, sprawled on my bed, the body of God.

You recognized it?

You bet. It shone.

Naked?

What I could see of it. Spindle legs.

You knew it was dead.

I didn't…I don't…I'm not—

You insist you could not see the whole body from the door because
these "others" blocked your view.

I do. The body lit the room like a moon.

You saw the feet.

Big as paddles. They hung over the bed like mine do.

How many "others"?

Maybe six. It's a small room.

They addressed you?

"We're angels!" one said. Like he had one of those boxes in his throat.

And you replied?

What could I say?

And these "angels" were undressing.

Clothes everywhere. Boots and underwear.

Male.

Both.

Both?

(evidence of splicing)

—and that's when he opened the window. The angel. The big one.

Naked.

It's crazy I know but yes. Stark. The room stank. They went straight to the bed.

And dragged you with them.

Uhuh.

Then you *could* see the entire body when you opened the door!

It shone. There was something under the skin—a light—a—a blood light.

But the sex—!

I told you I don't know. I couldn't see. They'd thrown my towel over the hips. The blue one.

(inaudible)

They?

Well someone! Before I got there.

We *know* you saw it.

But this is the body of God! Think of it!

Tell us what happened at the bed.

They were strong. We stood there
looking down. I was still wearing my hat.

At a corpse.

I told you no. Not—

(tape interrupted then resumes)

But in your drawings you place the angels at the bed and yourself
at the door.

They wore red ballet slippers—I remember now!

These are serious discrepancies!

I just wanted to see the face.

You saw the body. You saw everything!

I was dumbstruck. I mean my life's been so difficult of late, everything's fucked, the
whole planet, we're burning holes in the sky—

And yet you didn't notice the sex of God!

It was the business at the window.

Tell us again.

The room grows colder. "Lift the towel," the big one says, in that tin-can voice. I break
away to the window. Everything I've killed sits down there in the fresh snow looking up.

Everything?

Everything. Even the—

(garbled)

Were they threatening?

Who?

The dead.

God no. Just looking up through the falling snow. As if they might
speak. I remember thinking *so this is life!*

Didn't you speak?

Not a word.

Didn't you shout "Friends!"? Didn't you hold out the towel triumphantly?

The snow slow-swirling in the dark window. A skinny body. Gaunt.
The moonish light. My old blue towel over the hips. I remember the day
I bought it, it was my birthday and—

Did you lift it?

My mind was giving way. Do you understand? I expected…

Go on—

…a kind face.

You waved the towel! You cried out!

Already I was walking north—

Please, the truth!

Ahead in the trees my wasted years sang.

You saw everything.

It was weeks ago. Years.

You lifted it.

I lifted it.

Ah.

I was crying. The body whispered, I leaned in, I was very close, I could smell
wintergreen, I—

(remaining tape is not recoverable)

BROOMS

then like a dog I'll circle the yard, for days,
years, beneath the doomed trees, whatever it takes,
whimpering, yapping, fly-swarmed, in shadow, in sun,
resolutely scratching it down, each dirt-page eaten
by dust till the air swirls, ringing with bits of my life, the yammer
and howl, the snarls, the coupling, the menacing dreams,
I will hunker and watch, red-eyed, shivering, head swollen
with dreadful hymns, and as the nights cool and deepen
I will see him there, at my side, hands in his pockets, under
the trees, talking about the Virtues and the Questions and
the Ideas, and I am caught up, eager and hot like a boy,
even as I ask why we are such cruel weather upon the earth
and can neither live nor die in peace and he won't mock me
for my questions nor say that's life boy that's simply how it is
and we will walk easily and happily in the cold dark, under the
tall trees tossing, the two of us, the generations, and I will ask
again why the women disappeared, and all hope with them,
and why did we persecute them, beat and break and burn
them, age after age, fingering, fucking, swaggering in fear,
what *did* we fear, I can't remember, was it life, simply life—
and where have they gone, tell me, I beg, am I alone in a world
of men, men and money and death, in blood to our knees—
and won't he draw me to his chest, no words now, won't I
hear the great heart drumming under his double-breasted suit
and starched shirt, and won't I weep unashamed, him rocking me
and stroking my head before we turn back, my hand in his, silent,
grave, as dawn noses through the scrap piles—but no, no I'm alone,
as men should be, hunkered, watching the house, and it's not
likely he's in there, no I am sure he's not, the roof half gone, no
one is or ever was, I knew it as a boy, there is nothing but this,
the yard, the disemboweled cars, the empty house, the women
gone, and still, sir, I hold my ground, dogged, by a stack
of rotted tires, in the fresh shadows of the morning, unarmed,
unwashed, wondering which patch of dirt to smooth for my
stick, and what will I say, dear dead father, while Mother Sky
screams and the men take turns and the trees are blind brooms
rustling

ZERO YARD

I'm sorry, yes,
for the trouble, the mess—sorry

I'm late and shamed I reek
of song and death—sorry I flat

refuse
to mend my way

or shut
my mouth—though it's not

as if I haven't tried
to set it right—hurrying

in the dark
on the packed roads—

and damned if the house
isn't boarded up and the yard

stripped bare—no one to
gape, to gasp—you did

what?—as I hurl
my sorries at your door—

but a deal's a deal and yes, I
am sorry, so

furiously sorry, a penised
human shouting sorry I am

or ever bloody was!—bone
and flesh of me!—

sorry, mother! sorry, father!
sorry Sheriff Big!

that I called shame down
upon your house—a whole

heap
of sorry for having fouled the air—utterly,

damnably sorry
for these penitential stones

thudding against your door—deeply
and helplessly sorry

for the messy bed, the bad fuck—
and the squealing, lord! the

tears!—sorry
you had to hear this, now,

in the zero yard, in the silence
of the night

REUNION

I was cobbled from the junk of men.

Solange Garaban

I am calling them in, my selves, while I can, while light
and words abide, calling them home, if this ramshackle
house is home to anything except my voice, hoarse and half
mad, as if I were calling a lost child, or rousing the dead—Jed!
Jed!—and now at last they're coming, mobbing the road, filthy
yellow banners hollering ME IT'S ME THE REAL JED!—there's
Sideman, Singer, there's Prof and Licker, Mama's Boy and Uncle's Cunt,
and isn't that Keeper of Tears, shoulders slumped, in that godawful suit,
and right behind him Hipster fingerpopping, and jesus there's Whitey
and Tattler and King of the Dark, and back in the swirling dust
Little Bad Boy in Black with his bum bare, no ghosts these,
swaying and singing, such a din, Christ, grimed, grieving, each one
frantically wondering who in fuck is *that*, but all of them Jeds or Jebs or
Jubs, soiled, shamed, rude-boned and wildhaired, heartsick Fakes
and Flash-in-the-Pans, Bigot, Jerk, Critical Snob, all I have been, all
that I am, if I am anything at all but this gang of me crowding the chilly
skull, pressing, Dopester goofing in a swarm of gnats, Liar dragging
his sticky nets, Jed after Jed, straggling towards my call, my
bell and cry of amnesty, for Pianoman and Wasted Talent, for Cool
Fuck and Papa J, for Deadbeat Dad, for Privileged Male, selves boiling
out of the dusk like wasps, Jeds galore, I eat me, drink me, shit and piss
me, I kiss my stinking feet for mercy, I kiss my cock, for I am
all the men, the two-bit gods, manhandling the world, in my dream I
blister and split, faces leering out like the backs of spoons,
fuckups shouting at the falling dark as they surge houseward,
clambering over the trashed Buick and tire-heaps towards the porch
where I stand watching, my arms out, Jed the Rhymer, the Scribbler,
sure as all of us that I'm the real, the original Jed, the unsoiled little boy,
alone, crying hurry!—no tricks, no cameras hidden in my hair, I am all
you see, in my best suit, in this double dusk of time and light, while your
long legs still carry you, dragging your Books of Darkness, your alibis
and explanations, your resumes, from whatever hole or hovel life
drove you to, the vintage hells and remaindered heavens, a hundred
and one Jedediahs massing, muttering, moaning, and I
worry and pace, like a mother, Mother Jed, yet another self, who will
never abandon them, hoping that's not rain I smell in the underair
for where will they sleep, the dears, do I have enough blankets, enough

sweets, some dope, a *tuned* piano—and oh god what if they don't
recognize me and I really am alone at the heart of it all, doors
of the house banging, and what if Love does not come, walking
breathing Love, if Love can't find its way, is trapped somewhere, hurt
and unable to speak, or never heard my call, or finds us fouled beyond
repair, another Night of the Men, smoking, spitting, scared of everything
that moves—Hurry!—and while you're at it tell me just what Love can
say to men, to Jed, will one of you answer me, us, will you speak, the Love
I have never been but know better than I know myself, my selves, believe
me, the real man, the true Jed?

STABAT MATER

O quam tristis et afflicta
Fuit illa benedicta
Mater Unigeniti

At first I wanted to praise
—for the spectacle, you know,

the massy boulevards, the blare
of brass in the rinsed and shining air—

I had come to visit my dead
and talk to the poets, perhaps,

if they weren't too busy, and I'd play
a little piano to pay my way.

We never slept, the poets and I,
oh they were crazy days.

Now I'm back in town
and mobbed in my yard—

What's it like? Who'd you see?
—they pull at my clothes—

is there a list?—No, I say,
you don't understand

—I tap my head—it happens
here, beneath bone, in the dark

—*Enough!* they shout, don't fuck
with us, we saw you board the bus,

we ran your prints—we've got it
all—and they fan their pages—in

black and white—Wait! I
holler back, that's it! Heaven's

black, it's white, silent, birdless
—ok I was stretching it—though the guard

I blew in the shadows said
if you stay long enough things

take on a sheen of sorts—and sure
enough, as I was leaving, my mother

—that's her picture there, on the
cover—who had come to see me

off after our reconciliation—my mother,
who loved me, I'm certain, you could

see it in her eyes—stood
beneath the bare trees, tristis et

afflicta, my mother, we did not speak,
not once.

I remember the sweater draped
round her shoulders and pinned

with a gold hummingbird, it shone
such a dark and unforgiving blue.

THE BOOK

Someone is reading my book
aloud. Is it God?

Does God read?
And the voice—

a woman's voice but not
certainly not

my mother's who is dead.
Anyway isn't God a guy?

But if God's not reading my book
who is?

Maybe it's *God's* mother
who reads the Lives, while *he*

works the Malls,
pretending blindness.

My big beautiful book!

And the writing on the flyleaf
isn't mine. *Yea though I walk*

through the valley—some other Jed
or Jeb or Jub, wrote that. Nevertheless

the book exists. And surely someday God
will sit by the river

and open it. Dusk
will fall, the stars burn. Well,

he'll say, aloud
and throw his face

into his hands.

THE REAL QUESTION

You won't know me, not at first, if
in fact you show, it's late, I've changed, old
greasy coat, no underwear, hair falling out
while poem-spit dribbles
down my chin: oh no you won't be sure, dead
sure that what you see before you
in the dreaming door is what you've sought,
you call it Soul or Self or Higher Power—Good God!
and here it is, or I am, to hell with names
though neither they nor it nor I
intend you harm, we never have,
though we may have spooked
you, true enough, in the past, badly, you must
forgive us: how far Doubt drags us till we holler Stay!
But what *is* sure
is I'll unnerve you, like blood
blooming where it shouldn't: you'll stall
in the yard, stoned (still) and knocking
your heels till night descends
and your starry questions
rise, the old doozers, the dancers—Was darkness first?
Does God dream? Does Evil ever sleep?
Just what *is* justice anyway? Fork
on the right? Knife on the left? Huh?
Does anyone hear? Miserere! You are
so dear to me!
Still.
But it's your poem and you'll look
surprised, as if there were some other
life you'd rather live, though it's you
who called, you did, left hand
dialing while the right plays dumb, can we meet,
gotta talk, and I knew you were in the neighborhood,
sirens and fuckyous and shattering glass, the human
music, and now you're here, again, and I implacably
in front of you, I may even be inside, yes, high
in the skull lodge, that close, shawled in smoke

and smut, at the eye-caves peering out, watching
the street, trying to write it down without deceit,
with nothing but the plainest words and the small
music they sometimes make—your best voice, you know it,
booming but kind, cuffless, quavering,
whereas I can only scratch it here, on glassy air,
in dwindling light—shivering now and nothing, not
a sound, are you coming, you called, you
said it's urgent, damn it, who,
Who, ring it now with your whole voice, the real
question, the bone of it, the bloody bone, you've
got it, go on, at least, ask it, yes, jesus, is it
Love you want, is it Love in your face, Love waiting,
you calling, confused, confounded, cursing, it *is* urgent,
yes, can you see me, here, hands out, in the dark,
a beggar at your door—

II

ON THE BUS TO HEAVEN

IF YOU WERE HUMAN

Socrates: Well, then, what is a human being?
Alcibiades: I don't know what to say.

If you were human
you would understand

the hollering round the pit,
the suddenly sunlit bones.

And this business of home
and time *is* money

and bullets *sans doute* and probably
poetry too. Well I'll be ding-donged,

you'd mutter, bent under the hood—
That's life for you!

If.

And voices would gabble
under your clothes

and the mean air spoil
like meat and your hands

go for your own throat. Then up
at dawn, Heavens to Betsy

making sentences like bread.
You would do your years

in the Rabbit Shed and time
would seep from your shoes.

It's not for everyone, being human.

If you were instead a burrowing thing
and you slept in hollows and fed

on grubs and certain grasses and
tenderest shoots and were shy and

night-loving, knew nothing of words,
and did not carry

a miniature piano
under your tongue

and could not sing
or assemble, calculate

or curse, moved only
in the dark, came out

in the rain, left no
tracks, no spoor, avoided

mirrors and could
for a season live

on nothing at all
and saw no reason

to struggle up
from your knees to say

the damndest things, the
simplest things, impossible

things really—no reasons to
shudder

or change your underwear or
beg between the senator's knees—

no reason at all to gawk
or kneel or flee

pell-mell through the night
with mother clamped

like fury
in your hair—no reason,

I say, to sit
before the Book

and call the ancient curses
down upon the heads

of your enemies
whom you suspect

and rightly so
are everywhere,

in the yard
in the shadow

in the sentences that rise
like blisters from the page, like

veins on the backs
of the hands of God—

nor would you grope
—with what I can't deny

is desperation—grope,
I repeat, for words, for

music, some sort of song
to sing

in your troubled night—
if you were human

LITTLE SONG OF MEMORY

What was it I said, or did—or didn't?
Was God in His chair, was it night?

Did I say the wrong word, did I stutter
and burn—worse, did I speak at all?

And where were the others, family
and ghosts, the infamous Sheriff Big?

Was someone—anyone—there?
Enough! It's done, they're dead, yet

still I claw and howl at the dark
door. Christ, child, let it go. For

even if memory yields—says here
for what it's worth is how

it was and is—how will I know
what's real—for memories bicker

and deal, some staggering off in the
cold to die and others gnawed

by the rats of sorrow and shame
and all you can even hope to find

are bones—under your hair you hear
them clatter—bones of the mothers!

bones of the son!—black
bones of the words that bind them

ALMOST A LOVE SONG

I was in my best suit and circling His house, I'd been there for hours,
maybe years, in the cold drizzle, voices like wasps in my head, I was
dripping, dazed, my knees ached from the road, the hard macadam,

I was pacing the yard, the suck of my shoes in the mud, churning back
and forth between the disemboweled cars and gutted refrigerators, warped
boards and tumbled statuary, my coat yanked over my head against the

rain, I was gathering courage, girding up to knock but the porch was
deep, was spooky dark, then a 747 rumbled in over the river shaking my
bones and I cried Father!—like a boy—Father! it's me, my old face

shining under the trees—Over here, by the Buick!—wanting to tell him
I was well now but felt a stranger in the Land of Men and had this
recurring nightmare where I slogged through blood even to my knees

and hands, hands were grabbing my ankles—telling him how I kept
thinking my heart was dirty, like a smell you can't place so you keep
sniffing your armpits or your hands or down your shirt or is it your

feet or some sly fecal odor in the chair you rise from anxiously—I'd
always been dirty, inside, underneath, when all was said, and Father
knew everything, as though he'd screwed cameras into our skulls,

from the inside, surveiling eyes, blood-red LED's blinking, and he'd
stitched viewing screens into our palms and we could always see
ourselves seeing ourselves—eyes ad infinitum, always seen, watched,

weighed, ranked—so we'd keep our shoulders square, hands ready,
and no one could sneak up on us—Father it's me! it's—but the old
anger was on me that evening, in the dripping rain, shoes caked, no

cigarettes, the wet stink of me, the music of the road still droning
in my knees, every voice in me shouldering forth for a go, a sack
of gristly speech, I was shouting—someone was shouting—Father!

—pressing forward as I slogged toward the porch, past the white
Pinto sunk in the weeds, the windshield smashed, Father! I shouted,
he shouted, a red-faced boy in stop-time, his coat like a hood hiding

him, screaming Where in fuck were you these hundred years of
killing, off pulling your sorry pork with your cabbage fists, your
seed like a virus, every spilled gout a skillion men, battalions to

sweep and burn over the earth, whipping, raping—Father!—and I saw
that the door stood open and dark and shook in the gusting rain and the
rocker was empty but moving nonetheless and I could smell it again,

my heart, like a wet dog, or clothes buried in the woods, I sniffed my
hands but all I smelled was rain and all I heard was the jet scream
crunching the air, and I saw eyes flare in the shadows, maybe a cat

but He hated cats, no surprise, and I was still shouting what a bastard
He was, Sheriff Big, Captain Crunch, Head Hog, belching and
farting while gun smoke seeps from His fly, Death's pimp, gas bag,

His eyes two gobs of glue, the Chief, todopoderoso, Big Rapper
shaking His stiff stuff for bitches and ho's, good Christ, face like
bad meat, answer damnit, Oh King of the Fuck, answer you sorry

prick and I stood there hooded in the mud at the foot of the porch,
soaked, wheezing, my jaw still working but the words gone, the big
jet gone, my death like a bile in my throat—Father!—and Jesus what

was I doing, a man of fifty out there in the rain, in the night, his suit
sopping, hollering to himself, the neighbors aghast, the house
black as nothingness, His own house, God's house, the lie that won't

die, and another red-eye rocking in over the oily river, my hands
stretched out like a beggar's—I must tell Him, find Him to tell Him,
tell Him what, walking all this way, to finish in this trashed-out yard

—even as a kid I knew who He was, Father God, uhuh, oh Father God,
real as real, it was His world, He was the terrible boredom beneath
the snow, the sexual dread, the hump and hum of the mind—and there I

hulked, before the dark porch and even darker door, muttering in the
quickening rain, old and cold, hands dangling, a melodrama in a wet
suit, an old soul, stamping his feet—Father!—when someone, something

said *Wait* but I slobbered on, too furious to fear, like some schizoid Job
bellowing through the hiss of the rain—*wait*—*please*—and I stopped
stock still FOR WHAT I snapped, too stunned and miserable to wonder

was I hearing things, was I coming apart at last, my brain stumbling, too
much too little, too late—*I am Love*—OH LOVE I shot back, guffawing
and I'm Saint Fucking Francis in the Rain, slipping then knees smack

in the mud, look at my suit, jesus, and grabbing for the porch step—*I
am Love, I look after you*—YEAH WELL YOU CAN KISS MY—*I am not
God, I never said that*—and I lurched across the rotted boards

to the dark door—*I am everything good*—the voice right in my ear, I
slapped at my head, a dream, a nightmare—then I was in, at last, amazed,
out of the rain, and it was still, I could hear my breath and the rain

in the yard, I stood in the dark, listening, dripping, my heart drumming,
I shook like a dog, all these years and here I am, stumbling into the
kitchen, it was on me now, almost singing—*We are Love, you and*

I—dead flies on the table and rain swilling over the roof—*I can't do it
without you*—and I'm thinking I'll see a face if I just keep sane so I glare
into the shadows but nothing moves—DO WHAT—I say again and

all the time I'm filling with darkness, there's maybe an inch of light
left at the top, just under my hair, I'm too old for magic, for paranormal
peek-a-boo, just truth, that's all, a taste, a goddamn dime's worth

of truth tossed from the Great Lodge in the clouds, and I'm all mouth
again and furious, fuck this, fuck that, and all the time listening for
steps or the whirr of a tape machine and I barge through another dark

door—SHAZAM!—a table sits, a small lamp burns, then the voice—
this is the last room—and I'm hollering now, kicking at shadows
and punching the air, my mind derailed—SHOW YOURSELF!—

then I see the book on the table—*the last room*—DAMN YOU!—rain
spills from my hair as I bend and read—*I was in my best suit, I had my
years round my waist like money, I'd come from afar, walking the walk,*

I knew every mile of road, road home, road back, my knees ached, I'd
walked the nights, the days, tireless, singing and sobbing, I would find his
house, I would call out, in the rain, I would enter, I would rest—the rain

harder now and drumming the roof, the eaves streaming, I bend to the
book, all the poetry rushing under my hands, I am shaking in disbelief
and again the voice—*love is in the house tonight*—SHOW YOURSELF!

and I remember his breath on my head when I was a child and how
he scooped me into his arms, if he ever really did, in the father's house,
in my best suit, my best heart, my old and last suit, HOME—I say it,

I am home, but the house stands dark beside the even darker road, an
empty house, like the road, impossible empty and the voice is only my
own, a boy's voice, in the rain, a homeless voice, a moan, clumsy and

late, too late, like wind, like rain, like jet-wash, I turn, wanting out or
is it in—*love for you*—will I ever know, on a wet night, in the last room,
room of the house, my father's house, who is nowhere to be seen

ON THE BUS TO HEAVEN

All doomed day
we barrel

down the muddy road
our faces pressed

to the glass
and driver Hans

chugging his shame
and bellowing soon

meinem Damen und Herren
soon!

And what *is* Heaven
I ask the woman weeping

beside me—that old
dingdong

of Glory and Grace
our dead waving

in the bright grass—
Father! Sister! Brother! Friend!

Surely I say
gripping her hand

Heaven's a better life
each day a dance, a

poem, a kiss—better
than bloody this

THE HOUSE OF GOD

I've read it's high as Heaven,
the House of God,
maybe higher.

Its windows, edged in red,
outnumber the motherless dead.

And we know about the buses
idling in the haze below.

The fumes.

In my book, though,
it's the ruined shack I saw

as a boy and haven't
ceased to see, its occupant

—at least when I've peeped
through the window in back—

naked and picking his nose, or toes,
or preening his prick in a mirror.

I've never knocked
even on the coldest night

and when the wind is up
and the world too much

he sits to write: Dear Mother—

but when he presses on the page
fresh blood seeps out. He sniffs

his fingers—His? Hers?
Horrified, he flings his pen.

And the book—where did he put it?—
heavy, cold, his father's Book—

he grips his head and sings:

Where are my angels?
My Sunday suit and cigarettes?

What am I? What
are you? Are we

we? The mirror winks.
Mother of God, what to do?

BIRTHDAY

It's dawn
and I'm raking the yard and thinking
jesus I am

fifty-fucking-six and still
won't say
what I need to say—

when suddenly
BAP!
my parents drop

from the trees
like puppets
dragging

their dead toes
through my hair—while back
in the house the boy

pounds out boogie-woogie
on the parlor grand
and never hears the door

creak
as God
slips in—

Little Boy!
and hurling the rake
I scramble madly

for the house but my
old knees lock and Christ
I'm down, just as the kid

roars into *Honky Tonk Train*
and over my head
the puppets

jig and judder
—*Little boy!*—
and round us pale

angels rake up
darkness into piles
to burn

HERE THERE IS NO WHY

Every day I see my dead
in the pasture at dusk

perched on the hoods
of abandoned cars.

Why, I call
from the shoulder of the road

are we still at war?
Someone snickers.

And Heaven—is it
finished? Heh?

They light cigarettes and stare.

Why a penis, I persist,
or politics? Why psalms? Why books?

Why *my* mouth?
One of them opens his pants.

Another one turns, a woman.
Get over it, asshole.

They shamble off, some arm-in-arm,
singing

Hier ist kein warum, warum
Hier ist kein warum

Wait, I cry, lowering my rifle—
why not nothing—

nothing
at all?

A GOOD LIFE

Counselor:

I am writing my way into Heaven.
Who would have thought it?

What is Heaven?
Visualize, you'd coax,

the number 3 and
see it slip to 2 then

slim to 1
which droops

to loop
an oval doorway in the air—

What do you see?
and of course I saw

my suffering self
—or something like it—

crossing the field and God
or something like it

hailing from the edge
of uneasy woods

and the sun
like an old soul

sinking into the trees.
I saw, counselor, but could not say.

And now I write
the days and nights,

it's almost there, the real,
the right, the world

peeled back
and shining.

But what
if Heaven's writing me—

the muck, the prayers, the
grinding on?

ah this one, how shall we
write him—which

dreams, which sorrows and
regrets—look at him, this

human, in his muddy boots,
his teeth loose, his eyes

tear-bright, writing, he
insists, his way into Heaven

(plaint)

I am losing my words, is it winter, spring?
They steal away, in day or dark, my mind

collapsing in a clatter. I rummage
the rubble and—and—the word, damnit—

see?
Gone.

And mind you mark how Basic Being
—implacably there! —stick! stone!—

now drifts the rain-slick roads like ghosts
growling—*Give us back our names.*

What *can* one do with them, words—
how say *no,* or the all-important *why,*

or—or—weeping Christ—how, in short
can I tell you I love you? (I do!) How

will I even *think*—my sentences slipping
like wreckage down the snowy slope—

how *choose*—left, right, flee, fight—
eh? How cry for bloody help?

Give them back, my words, they'll
sound all wrong in another's mouth.

Give them back and I'll curse you
in couplets and kiss your—your—

(   )
and tell you who you are and how

precisely how
the world will end

NIGHT PAGES

When I was young
I burned to write.

I wrote my father
up from the dead.

Dark doors slammed,
my pencil throbbed.

I wrote for god
and the hood

and the Nothing hunched
in my heart. I wrote

that little song of shame
you sing to stay the dark.

Love circled the house
but how could I hear

in that roar of words?
I wrote. I died.

My pages swirled away
and stuck

in the dirty trees.
Tell them in Heaven

it wasn't right. Tell them
in Hell, I never said no,

at night.

MUSE

Muse? But mine is not amused.

Solange Garaban

You know the tale
how Muse showed up

but you were drunk
or high or out

or cranking your tunes
or weeping or

wanking—whatever it was you were
not there, knock-knock, nothing—no

light in the kitchen, no turned-down
bed or cookies or cats

on the couch—just shadow and dust,
just flies.

And Muse walks in, shoeless
and smacking her gum

or shriveled, humped, she limps, she
lisps—maybe it isn't a woman at all

but a dude in a suit
and alligator boots, *I used to dance*

boys while clocks tick
in his mouth and his hair

reverberates—and seeing
the smoking lamp, the tipped-over

chair, the opened book, he writes,
she writes—*too late! too late!*

across the mirror in lipstick
or maybe even blood.

And had you stayed? Undid
the lock, trimmed the lamp,

turned left
then right, said this and

never mentioned *that*
and chose a brighter shirt—oh

had you
cleaned it up, nixed

the jokes, zipped your fly,
criminy JUST STRAIGHTENED UP

and scrubbed your tongue
and made those windows

shine—what then? Story's
done before begun, Muse

will say with a tight smile
and time's a nasty thing.

THE VISITATION

They'll appear in the door, no trumpets, no fuss,
a hand on my arm, a nod, a look, and of course
they know, they've always known, and haven't I—
it was only a question
of time, it is always a question of time, and what
was I thinking
for one cannot in the end resist
the truth—I was not
what I seemed, not at all, I was always
pretending—oh maybe a moment here,
or there
but who was I fooling, all these years—a life!—my
god how arrogant of me to think
I could be other than in fact I am,
by nature, or is it fate, take your pick but surely
doomed to be what they said in fact I was
and would always already be, a sham, a fake—
poseur, corrupt and corrupting, duplicitous,
rude—in short a shit, a cheat, sad Dasein,
who talked his way in and sometimes
out, untested, no Latin, no Greek—
and they'll haul me off, my students
crowding the door to see, and
point me into the dark, and watch me
shuffle off, head bowed—
what could we do, he gave us no choice—
and back in their rooms they'll kick their shoes
in the corner and fall
across their beds, and the night will ring once more
with the songs
of the just

KYRIE ELEISON

Lord.
Someone!
Have mercy on us.

One angel calls
and calls again.
Another struggles.

This angel shrugs
and ambles off into the corn.
That angel carries a stick

thick as my wrist.
Whoa. Of course
they are wingless

and squinty and speak
if at all
only when spoken to.

This angel spits at my feet.
Hey I say.
This angel sits my chest and stares.

What? Why?
This angel says boo.
This angel carries letters from the dead

in a language I cannot read.
The smallest angel opens the piano.
Sit.

The angel in the wig wants to talk.
Another walks straight through me.
This angel—*this* angel—

who are you,
so out of breath,
and nothing on your feet?

A SHORT LIFE OF SHERIFF BIG

He was dragged out of the mother's house—
tied to the back of a horse galloping
backwards into the Land of Men.

Solange Garaban

I was a boy when the call came.
I caught the High Noon train.
Goodbye, Father. Oh Mumsy, Wiedersehen!

And how I grew, buff and beau,
wading in blude (mimes) and warrior woe.
Truth!—they say I said—and so?

(he shakes his black-hatted head)

Sir! we barked, in shadow and sun.
Sir! when the Suck was done
and the terrors begun.

Then grizzled did we sweep
down upon them in their sleep,
the fuckers, marvelously did we make them weep.

(he adjusts his hat)

Now my knees dread
and my dick's dead.
Every morning I spread

my cheeks. SIR!
SIR!
Oh sir.

THE FIRST LESSON

Don't be surprised
when out of the storm
they shoulder in
their soaked coats
sweeping the floor
and the rain
hissing behind them—

Don't stare
at their razored hair
and their eyes
which shine
from the bottoms of time
and their soiled feet
which make no sound—

Don't flinch
when they shout
It is Written!
nor shut the doors
behind you as you
take them room
to room, foolish child—

Don't gasp
when they yank
long knives
out of their mouths
and slash your bed
and cut their names
in your table top—

Don't shudder
when they rut
on the rug
at your feet
then stagger up to pitch

your furniture
into the dark—

Don't whimper
when they pry
your fingers back
till they snap
and piss your feet
and shit your head
and cave your mouth in—

Don't lose control
when they shoulder out
singing, the sound
of their song soft
through the hissing rain
as they gain the muddy
hill behind the house—

Oh do not despair
for they are men, child,
and they are written
and that—
surely that—
is the first lesson.

REAL ANGELS

Say what you will
about angels—it was all

we could do
not to drop our cameras

in the dust and go.
And drop and go

we did. It wasn't
what we pictured—

is it ever?—yet
it was everything we asked

and more, I swear—
the heart, the whole. Oh

it was wrong—you think
we didn't know?—

but we were so
far from our mothers

and hadn't our fathers,
bless them, blazed the way?

But when we saw them
descending in the haze

over the old ball field
their robes billowing

up and their long
members and pinkish

testicles like clapper and bell
and everyone pointing

and shouting and spreading
their banners in the hot grass—

Thank God, one read,
We have suffered enough!

and their white hair
streaming as they fell

or floated
for their coming down

outlasted light—real
angels, mother, in the dusk

and hungry, they announced,
as bears—

BLOOD CLOCK

I

When, you ask, you push, you pry, when this, when that—when I was
young, when I was—what, what—when I saw God-in-the-Bushes, I
was five, no, six, it was cold, it was bright, I suppose, I guess—*think,
damnit!*—was it then, is it now, what city, what month, nail it down *I
can't remember,* God-in-the Bushes unzipped, his laugh like a swamp
in his throat

II

—it was when I was always lying, yes, to whom, to her, to you, bushes
of lies, always sniffing my fingers, I cannot stop, cannot start, the smell
of Him, like old shoes, Vitalis, corruption—when I wore boots, had crabs,
stuttered, even in prayer—stu-stu-stu—I have always prayed, under it all
jesus when, when, where—

III

what about where, was it in the shed, in the cellar, on the sour bed, was it
after or before, before what, *I can't remember*—where, when, you see how
it goes, I was five, six, what was I wearing, were there words, I met Time
in the flesh, Time in the bushes, God-time twitching and blind, is that not
enough for you, how could I speak, what could I say, I swallowed the
clock, greasy time, son of the father, an old tale in the world of men

IV

good Christ why call it up, life's short enough—for whom? for what?
—what matters when, or where, to hell with why, it's down the years
I roll, strung tight, bloody-gummed, bingeing and purging, remembering
nothing, hunting my death, blowing out the lamp, my father's lamp,
always a child, speechless in time, the mocking tick, the sneering tock
—*where is my father's lamp*—?

V

when, where, you expect me to know, how it all began with God-in-the-
Bushes, I was five, maybe six, is that enough, fuck time, it's saved and
damned, there, where, in the bushes of the mind, it was April, it was Easter,

yes, in '47, I'm sure, certain, it was risen, head in hand, but why then, why
now, for the hundred thousandth time, I ask you, why that song and dance
and all the time you watching, pushing, prying, *God sees every little thing you
do,* in the bushes

VI

this reek of memory, like singed hair, like ass, and the mouth, wet, slack,
the cavern of why, the Johnny Walker breath—details, details—why these
words and not yours, the pretty ones, the poetry words, the sly lines and
gorgeous turns, lift it into art—*what's the dirtiest word you know—that's
my poem,* in my teeth like a ratchet, or a bearing gone, here, in the bushes,
in the make-believe

VII

time's up, time's out, the clock's in fib, when, when, the hair, the spit, the
swollen veins of ends and means, the grunt, the gasp, where, why, why in
fact remember that, in all the shadow and all the sun, why something, why
anything at all, the road's old, mother, the sky full of church, my head heavy
with all the books, the poems, the songs, still there, still a boy, little fuck
dog, all whys, whats, wheres and whens, why call it back, the laughing god,
the clock in my blood, time in the bushes, the sting of His hands *hold still boy*
the smell of it, the words, the worlds, *hold still,* in man-time, as my knees
moan, pushing through the drear, soul adrift, hi-ing and bye-ing

VIII

think—it was spring, ok, in my Easter suit, church day and hadn't He
risen, the Kyros, the King, *little bunny boy,* when He wound my clock,
tick of my blood, tock of bone, I could not hold, I was nothing, nothing
at all, a mop of curls, a pinkbrown eye, a stutter, a stink—*think*—when
He lit his Lucky Strike and ashes caught in His belly hair and He spat
between my checks and ground His teeth and I tumbled slo-mo down
the lightless shaft of time, the fall that binds, turning, knees drawn up

IX

oh when, oh where, why now, thou sayest it, the clock grinds on, a wind
in the bushes, time's dark bells bonging when, where, why, in the world
beneath my hair, His hands in my hair, when I was a child, mother, when
I was grown, timeless, placeless as smoke, an animal speck, in the tumble
and rush

X

when, a way in, a way out, a crossing, a black bridge back to the bushes
where you first saw God, the rogue Father, the Master, winding the blood-
clock, zipper down, for time's sake, time present, time past, you know the
song, time and its racket of slamming doors, when to where to why, slam,
slam

XI

at the end of day, when I tap the word *freedom* and it rings the dark
down, when I stand in the yard and love the ruined earth, like a child,
always a child, when I hear my body, it's trying to speak, trying to say, to
mean, when I know, when I rise in the windy dark, rise in the bushes,
the terrible bushes, watching, touching, and I am forever when and
irrevocably where and fatefully why, sweet why, in the light of dead
stars sifting down through the trees

XII

when, when, when I was young, when I was fair, when I was—what,
what—when I saw God-in-the-Bushes, the beginning of time, the First
Tick, the birth of when, the crying out, his laugh like a swamp in his throat

LITTLE SONG

Master today is my last.
I've put everything back in the box.
My rage—what was I without it?
and my cock and my tongue
and of course the Book—are you
listening—and the Stick, stuffing
them in, name, shame and
comings apart—oh
and me mum!
and my daddy's ghost! Everything I don't
remember but should, my place, my time, my
guilt—the tears!—and last, oh last, my love
for Thee, Master I am pushing it down
with my hands, the powerful hands of a pianist,
Master I am climbing in,
I am pulling it shut.

THE KINGS OF MY COUNTRY

Je vous écris du bout du monde

Henri Michaux

My love—what can I tell you?

Our new king has no kingdom.
He does not know this.

We are written on his body
where he cannot see. Trust me

he snaps with a clap on the back.
What was it

you used to say—you can't eat
soup with a fork! Yet I admit

we sometimes catch ourselves
at windows holding our breath.

What is it we fear? A king's
a king. He likes his wine and

meat. Yet word has it he's
chaste. Imagine. And what

will become of Beget and Begot?
He says we have much to fear

in Sheriff Big and the dissolution
of order. Order indeed. We wonder,

too—and not a little—about the
steady disappearance of birds on

palace grounds. And the edicts—
full of grammatical errors—which

shut our cities down for weeks.
Good things? Well

there's plenty of fresh bread.
We shout NO! on the street

and no one hauls us off. Naturally
we would like to speak with him,

our new king—share a fire
and meal but all day he rides

in his dark car along the borders
on empty roads with more guards

than I can count. There is
talk of course. No one knows,

for example, where he's from, he
simply appeared, poof, proclaiming

himself our King. We had no reason
to doubt—his impeccable speech, his

carriage—how he strode
the boulevards, hatless, as if

he knew us all, had always
known us and had our best

interests at heart, the fullness
of life. But we scarcely see him now

and though we're fat with bread
and travel in our vehicles freely

and at unnerving speeds, and great
white discs scan our heavens

for revelations we could never
have imagined before the installation

of our King—still, as I said
there's the business of the birds

and add to that the shuttered
shops and long gray sheds

going up in the fields behind
the abandoned school, and the

smell, the smell—how to
describe it, a sweetness

with a secret as my neighbor
puts it, which nevertheless

is in our clothes and in our
skin as we know too well

lying in each other's arms
these winter nights most of which

feel longer and darker
than we even remember them being.

Thus one might say we have our
questions, our worries and

hesitations, and are always
expecting an announcement

or proclamation of some sort
in the papers or on the televisions

which of course are everywhere,
even on the streets, at regularly

spaced intervals, those flickering
screens showing us mostly

ourselves as we pass or pause
or sit to bury our face in our hands—

in any case I'm fine, really, I simply
didn't know I would find your

question about our new King
so damnably difficult to answer,

as if I'd never thought of it
before, the kings of our country,

there have been so many, as you
well know, and we have always

talked about them, in the workplace,
at school, at home, and why

should it be different now, is it
our age, the bad air, the punishing

heat, the drought, the failed banks,
the general hush over the country,

the withered corn, the morose
and incessant wind?

What do you think?
Who is your King

in these dark years?
And why do they

continue to delay
your papers for travel?

LITTLE SONG II

Knowing now how
little I know
and grasping
how thoroughly
and in what
everlasting dark
I am lost—
and having prayed as everything that lives
prays
with spitty grief
and terrored heart
to what or whom
I could not say or ever
why
but surely
to no avail—
and having reached
at last
with mind undone
heart's door—
what to do
but give
to you
my hat
my stinky shoes
and stout stick
and with my
shadow slung
across my back
go off
down the good road
singing

Notes

The phrase "Zero Yard" is borrowed from the book *Falling in Love Falling in Love with You Syntax,* by the poet Sheila Murphy.

The fragment—

O quam tristis et afflicta	Oh how sad and afflicted
Fuit illa benedicta	was that blessed
Mater Unigeniti	Mother of the only begotten

—is taken from the Stabat Mater traditionally attributed to Jacopoda da Todi (d. 1306). I recommend listening to the Estonian composer Ärvo Pärt's setting of the poem.

"Blood Clock" is a phrase I read, I believe, in the diaries of the painter Paul Klee. I cannot remember the specific source.

About the Author

Jed Allen was born on the potholed road between Heaven and Hell and he walks there still. His writing has appeared in numerous journals and in *Fever Dreams: contemporary Arizona poets* (Univ. of Arizona Press). He has raised goats, worked as a janitor, cut and sold firewood door to door, made adobes, and is an improvisatory pianist and bassist. He teaches a variety of writing classes at Phoenix College and has also directed their Creative Writing Program. Across his back he has written: *todos somos ilegales.*